"I use the original *Notice Notes* with our
Social Justice Focus Group, a group of RAs
who want to dig deeper into these issues.
They love the examples and it gives us
plenty to talk about during our
30-minute meetings."

Tom Hicks
Associate Dean of Students
Coe College

Still Noticing

Notice Notes II

A Reflection Journal

Compiled by:
Jessica Pettitt

This Journal belongs to:

Table of Contents

Foreword We are living in a time of great change. It is exciting to see how much progress has been made over the last 50 years. We've just celebrated the 50th anniversary of the National March on Washington for Jobs and Freedom, and many would say we have come a long way and that the dream has been achieved. While I agree we've come a long way, I would also say, "we've got a long way to go."

Notice Notes invites us into the dialogue with self and others about just how far we have come. I have come to value *Notice Notes* because of what I experience as "Oppression Novocain."

Novocain is a numbing agent that keeps the body from feeling the intensity of pain. Most often one would experience Novocain in the dentist office. Novocain makes the process of having deep dental work easier to bear. I believe we are all being given "Oppression Novocain" so that we won't feel the pain of the work that still needs to be done.

What does Oppression Novocain look like?

- We are in a post-racial society.
- A black man has been elected President.
- There are more women CEOs than ever before.
- Most people in the country support gay marriage.
- Everybody loves Oprah.
- Ellen was given her own daytime talk show and starred in mainstream makeup commercials.
- There are queer people on prime time.
- Gay marriage has received wide support from the President of the United States as well as many other political officials.
- We no longer say Merry Christmas; we say "Happy Holidays."
- We have gender-neutral bathrooms in the new building or resident halls.
- We have interpreters for all conference programs.
- Our voicemail is now in English and Spanish and Spanish is first.
- We invited Jessica Pettit, Jamie Washington, Kathy Obear, Vernon Wall, becky martinez, Sam Offer, Tim Wise, Maura Cullen…to our campus last year; therefore, we get diversity and social justice.
- Others….

These are just a few examples of what "Oppression Novocain" looks and sounds like. It is important to remember that the intention of Novocain is not to do harm, but to ease pain. However, the reality is that Novocain only masks the pain. "Just because I don't feel it, does not mean nothing is going on."

Notice Notes invites us to let the Novocain wear off. It challenges us to see what we have not been seeing in ourselves as well as others. It is important to note that when Novocain begins to wear off, it does not feel good. Many of us seek other pain management options so that we never have to feel the intensity of the procedure that we just experienced. Thus, I encourage you to let yourself feel the pain. Allow yourself to ache from the realities of our need for ongoing work. Allow that pain to move you into self and community action. Don't run away from it.

I invite you to use *Notice Notes* as a tool for reflection, self-work, and change.

Notice difference and allow it to matter.
Observe the dynamics at play in like groups
     and across difference.
Track the patterns that support marginalization.
Investigate through the lens of difference
     for deeper learning.
Consider the possibility that oppression
     is playing out.
Engage yourself and others to create positive change.

The Work Continues;

Rev. Dr. Jamie Washington
President, Washington Consulting Group
Founding Faculty, Social Justice Training Institute
8331 Scotts Level Road, Baltimore, MD 21208
Office: 410-655-9556 Fax: 410-655-9793
Cellular: 443-794-1547
Website: www.washingtonconsultinggroup.net

Acknowledgements

I didn't know when I started compiling the first edition of *Notice Notes* that there would be a second edition. Literally, a calling from users of the first edition led to the compilation of this second edition. I would like to thank those facilitators for stirring up an incredibly important conversation.

Hannah Lozon also deserves acknowledgment here. Through thick and thin, stress and down time, illness and health, you have always been a supporter and challenger of me and my work. Thank you, friend.

Special thank you to Lush Newton for your artwork and inspiration.

I would like to thank the Social Justice Training Institute (SJTI) Listserv community for assistance, support, and learning opportunities yet to come. I also need to thank Maura Cullen, Jamie Washington, Kathy Obear, Vernon Wall, and becky martinez, the founders and faculty of SJTI, for providing me with a space to begin my own work as a white woman doing anti-racism work. I hold myself responsible for the work I did in that space and the work I continue to do.

Ten percent of all profits from the sales of *Notice Notes* will be given to SJTI, Inc., to continue and support the work done in the professional institutes, student experiences, drive-in trainings, and other community initiatives. To register for the next SJTI Institute, visit:

www.sjti.org

For suggested readings, visit:
http://sjti.org/suggested_reading.html

Note to Reader

Notice Notes is designed to be open enough for you to do what you need to do with it. If you need support along your journey, then please feel free to contact me for a helping hand, listening ear, or even a virtual or physical hug.

If you have observations that you would like to share for future editions of *Notice Notes*, please send an email to contactme@iamsocialjustice.com. To continue the conversation, visit www.iamsocial justice.com or call (917) 543-0966.

Know that we are doing the best we can with what we have — everyone is doing the best they can with what they have. Provide yourself and others with this humanity. That is what gets me out of bed each morning.

Always,

Jessica Pettitt

Jess

If Not Us, Then Who?

As I continue my work of self-reflection and stirring up conversations around the country, I find that I, and my audiences, still need inspiration or motivation to step up.

"If Not Us, Then Who?" comes from a combination of James Larkin and a Hopi Prophecy. James Larkin's memorial reads, "The Great Appear GREAT Because We Are on Our Knees. Let's Rise." The Hopi Prophecy that I am referring to is, "We Are the Ones We Have Been Waiting For." Together... I think this is the ultimate inspired source of motivation.

We know there is problem. We are wasting time looking for others to be the solution. We — I/You/We — are the answer.

Now — back to work!

How to Use Notice Notes

We take in stimulus using our senses. We may touch, taste, hear, smell, or see information as well as use our intuition, gut feelings, past experiences, and ideas to make literal sense. How one makes sense of a situation may vary from time to time, or there may be a favored process of taking in a given experience. This is personal and ever-changing for some. I ask in this space that you take information in and then reflect upon how you might make sense of it, and why. Record your observations or your noticings and reflect on your own experiences to uncover or highlight patterns of reactions, inactions, and actions.

Noticing[1] is an objective recording or acknowledgement of an event, free of judgment, explanation, logic, excuses, or reasoning.

Recording your observations can be done in prose, incomplete thoughts, drawings, word mapping, or whatever form you are comfortable using to articulate your observations both external and internal.

Reflection relies on the observer or noticer to engage in a dialog internally or with others with the purpose of discovering patterns, roots, and ways of showing up.

Privilege is an inherited and/or earned power within a dominant group membership that may not be blameworthy but does come with a degree of responsibility. The socially constructed dominant identity is dependent on the oppression of a/many subordinated identities.

It is my belief that undertaking self reflection from a position of one's dominant identity(ies) is a less costly/risky path towards change because those identities are the actual source(s) of power.

Reflection Prompts

What emotions am I feeling right now?

When do I feel safe and what do I notice?

When do I feel scared and what do I notice?

When do I feel intimidated (due to something I can sense — or not sense) in a situation where oppression is playing out?

What do I do or not do?

When do I talk too much? Why?

When am I silent? Why?

When do I cry? Why?

Why am I reacting this way?

What would I do/feel if I were one of the people in this noticing?

What would I do/feel if I were yet another person in this noticing?

What variables could change that would elicit different reactions/inactions on my part?

What is the pattern of my noticings?

What do I not notice?

Within these patterns, what covers up the root of my feelings?

What experiences do I cover in similar ways?

What do I use as a cover up? Excuse?

Where do I place responsibility?

When do I fix a situation?

When do I confront a situation?

When am I more comfortable confronting injustice?

When am I not?

How do I protect others with my privilege?

When do I protect myself with my privilege?

Who do I judge?

How do I forgive others?

How do I forgive myself?

What keeps me in the struggle when the end is not in sight?

Reaction/Inaction Patterns

As you reflect, every once in a while turn back and see if you can uncover patterns of your reactions or inactions. When do you respond in a "heady," "hearty," and/or "action"-orientated manner? Are there differences in your response behaviors based on what kind of power dynamic is at play? I bet there are! I also bet that depending on your identities and lived experiences — there will be patterns there too!

 HEADY

If you respond with questions or find yourself with a heightened need for additional information, you are having a heady response. Sometimes, you may need your questions answered before you can think about anything else. There are both good and bad things associated with a heady response.

 **HEARTY**

A hearty response is an emotional response. Regardless of whether you are feeling for the characters in the prompts or experiencing your own emotions — new or relived — this is a hearty response. There can be advantages and disadvantages to a hearty response.

 ACTION

Ever leap into action before you know all the details? This is an action-oriented responder classic move! If you are filled with a need to "do" something in response to a prompt or the need to "do nothing" then you are in full-on action mode. Paralysis to petitions are common action responses. There are lots of pros and cons to action responses.

CRUCIBLE! MOMENTS

After you figure out your "go-to" response, you may also determine your #2 response. It is the responses from your #3 place that are your crucible moments in life. These experiences will forever alter your character and how you behave or respond in the future. This is the gift of Noticing.

Week 1 Black students at the University of California, San Diego worry about targeted violence (physical or verbal) after multiple racially charged incidents occur in the span of a few weeks. The first incident was the public display of a noose in the library.[2]

_____

_____

_____

_____

_____

_____

_____

_____

_____

Week 2 The Lesbian, Gay, Bisexual, Transgender (LGBT) Resource Center at the University of California, Davis decided not to remove derogatory and hateful vandalism from the front door to educate the community about the real experiences of the LGBT community on campus. The statement issued included, "Erasing it makes it possible to avoid believing these things happen on our campus." [3]

_____

_____

_____

_____

_____

_____

_____

Week 3 In March 2012, Norrie, an Australian citizen, made gender history when the New South Wales government legally recognized Norrie as neither a male nor a female, but as "non-specified." [4]

Week 4 After being harassed by trolls with hateful and profane posts, the website Racebending.com's Facebook page was taken down for breaking FB's terms of agreement. Site administrators attempted to manage the negative attacks and challenged FB for its response.[5]

_____

_____

_____

_____

_____

_____

_____

_____

_____

_____

Week 5 Protestors from the Westboro Baptist Church won an appeal based on freedom of speech after picketing at a fallen Marine's funeral in celebration of American soldiers dying. The surviving family had been awarded $5 million dollars in damages by a jury. The case is now in front of the Supreme Court.[6]

_____

_____

_____

_____

_____

_____

_____

_____

Week 6 Members of the University of California Board of Regents and UC's President apologize and take responsibility for the realities faced by minority students on campus. One Board member, Eddie Island, stated, "We as a board failed to provide a nurturing environment. We didn't intend to, but we have failed."[7]

_____

_____

_____

_____

_____

_____

_____

_____

_____

Week 7 In April 2012, most U.S. hospitals (those receiving Medicare and Medicaid payments) followed an instruction from President Obama and his Health and Human Services Secretary to allow all patients the right to designate their own visitors and those who they wish to consult at crucial moments. These facilities cannot deny these privileges based on race, national origin, sex, sexual orientation, gender identity, and/or disability.[8]

_____

_____

_____

_____

_____

_____

_____

Week 8 The Chico, California, Police Department called the stabbing of Joseph Igbineweka on April 18, 2010, a hate crime. Igbineweka, the student body president of the local university, was walking home alone when he was followed and threatened with racial slurs by two males. He was then stabbed multiple times.[9]

_____

_____

_____

_____

_____

_____

_____

_____

Week 9 Residents in Arizona can sue cities if they perceive that a new law, SB1070, isn't being enforced. This law mandates that anyone who is "reasonably suspicious" should be questioned as if he or she is an undocumented immigrant or inside the U.S. without authorization. Also, immigrants not carrying immigration papers can be charged with a state crime.[10]

_____

_____

_____

_____

_____

_____

_____

_____

Week 10 While a transman was in the men's bathroom at California State University, Long Beach, he heard his name and turned; he was immediately attacked by a man who used a knife to cut the word "it" across the transman's chest.[11]

_____

_____

_____

_____

_____

_____

_____

_____

_____

Week 11 All Ethnic Studies programs were banned in April 2010 in the state of Arizona because they "advocate ethnic solidarity instead of the treatment of pupils as individuals."[12]

_____

_____

_____

_____

_____

_____

_____

_____

_____

_____

Week 12 In the 1990s, hundreds of Spanish-speaking teachers were recruited by the state of Arizona and hired as part of a broad-based bilingual education program. As of 2000, those with "heavy or ungrammatical" accents must meet strict English standards or they will be fired or reassigned. They are offered a limited time to take classes to meet the standards.[13]

Week 13 The Governor of Wisconsin in May 2010 signs a new bill SB 25, which allows the state superintendent of public instruction to ask schools to change race-based teams, mascots, logos, and nicknames that promote discrimination, harassment, or stereotyping.[14]

_____

_____

_____

_____

_____

_____

_____

_____

_____

A residence hall at the University of Texas has a new name: Creekside Resident Hall. This new name replaces the original name honoring a law professor who also served as a Ku Klux Klan Leader in Florida. The change is made to be in line with current university core values. [15]

_____

_____

_____

_____

_____

_____

_____

_____

Week 15 A spoof ad campaign called "American Able" brings visibility to the realities of all women and not just the thin and able-bodied. The campaign mocks the highly sexualized images of American Apparel ads.[16]

_____

_____

_____

_____

_____

_____

_____

_____

_____

_____

Week 16 The American Academy of Pediatrics (AAP) encourages its members to be prepared to navigate conversations with parents who may be accustomed to a cultural practice involving ritual cutting or alteration of the genitalia of females. The AAP "opposes all types of female genital cutting that pose risks of physical or psychological harm, counsels its members not to perform such procedures, recommends that its members actively seek to dissuade families from carrying out harmful forms of FGC, and urges its members to provide patients and their parents with compassionate education about the harms of FGC while remaining sensitive to the cultural and religious reasons that motivate parents to seek this procedure for their daughters." [17]

_____

_____

_____

_____

Week 17 After receiving public complaints, an artist is asked to "lighten" skin tones in a large public mural in Prescott, Arizona.[18]

_____

_____

_____

_____

_____

_____

_____

_____

_____

_____

Week 18 Peace activists giving aid to Gaza were attacked by armed Israeli commandos and defended themselves with chairs and sticks.[19]

_____

_____

_____

_____

_____

_____

_____

_____

_____

_____

Week 19 An ex-husband creates a blog about "creative" ways to use his ex's wedding dress. This blog goes viral and leads to his wife being aggressively contacted from different media sources requesting an interview. The wife is embarrassed and humiliated and concerned about the attention this issue is getting and how it is impacting the former couple's two young children at school.[20]

_____

_____

_____

_____

_____

_____

_____

Week 20 White male westerners are hired by a Chinese company to wear suits and tour its facilities as a way to increase perceived credibility.[21]

_____

_____

_____

_____

_____

_____

_____

_____

_____

_____

Week 21 In 2010, the Supreme Court ruled 5-4 in support of anti-bias policies on campuses related to campus-based organizations that promote discrimination under the guise of freedom of religion. All student organizations must follow campus non-discrimination policies.[22]

_____

_____

_____

_____

_____

_____

_____

_____

Week 22 A Center for Men's Leadership and Service at the College of Saint Benedict & Saint John's University aims to "create a safe and respectful environment for students to share their stories and discern who they are... for both men and women to explore the masculine condition, foster personal and spiritual growth and raise awareness of the consequences of gender roles... together we seek to work for justice and better the lives of men and women through innovative programs, scholarship and service." [23]

_____

_____

_____

_____

_____

_____

_____

Week 23 After a round of phone interviews for a Resident Director position, the top candidate is invited to an on-campus interview. The candidate responds that she wants to come to campus, but isn't able to travel at the moment. She goes through another round of phone interviews and ends up being offered the position. She accepts and then immediately informs the Director of Residence Life that she is eight months pregnant and would miss training and the first few months of the semester. The Director rescinds the job offer.

_____

_____

_____

_____

_____

_____

For CNN's AC360, Margaret Beale Spencer reenacted in 2010 a landmark study from the 1940s that measured the effects of segregation and racial bias in young children. The participants in the 2010 study were white and black children from New York and Georgia. The study confirmed that little has changed regarding the positive bias associated with white dolls and the negative bias associated with black dolls.[24]

_____

_____

_____

_____

_____

_____

_____

Week 25 Transwomen are now allowed to play for the LPGA as players no longer need to be "female at birth." [25]

_____

_____

_____

_____

_____

_____

_____

_____

_____

_____

_____

Week 26 At Miami University, the 68th annual "Indian Party" invites participants to "get dressed up like your favorite Indian and pow wow around the keg" and "get wrecked... you know Squanto would." [26]

_____

_____

_____

_____

_____

_____

_____

_____

_____

_____

Week 27 The media didn't cover a recent act by Denzel Washington and his family during a visit to the troops at Brooke Army Medical Center in San Antonio, Texas. This facility works specifically with burn victims. The families of the victims stay at Fisher Houses — family-like hotels that are almost always at full capacity. After a tour, Washington asked how much was needed to build a new facility for more family members to be able to stay; he then wrote a check for the amount on the spot.

_____

_____

_____

_____

_____

_____

Week 28 The play *Hairspray* explores issues of integration and racial tension.

The theater department of a majority white college in Iowa wants to produce the play and the director targets the small community of color for new actors.

_____

_____

_____

_____

_____

_____

_____

_____

_____

Week 29 A mother decided to send her children to a higher-ranked neighboring county's school where their grandfather was a resident. After four years, a county school official said the mother was, "cheating because her daughters received a quality education without paying taxes for it," pursued charges, and prevailed. The mother is currently in jail.

_____

_____

_____

_____

_____

_____

_____

_____

Week 30 A local café is run by volunteers and serves organic and local meals every day. Customers pay what they can afford and those who can't pay eat for free. The anonymous payment box covers about 75 percent of the expenses and the rest is provided through donations and grants. [27]

_____

_____

_____

_____

_____

_____

_____

_____

Week 31 Colby Bohannan, an Iraq War Veteran and Texas State University student, started an organization called Former Majority Association for Equality in response to the difficulty he experienced in finding scholarships. FMAE offers grants "exclusively to Caucasian men" due to their "disadvantage when applying for college scholarships." [28]

_____

_____

_____

_____

_____

_____

_____

_____

Week 32 The 2010 census shows that since 2000, when census data was first gathered on mixed race or multiracial children, the population of these children is growing significantly faster that previously estimated. The population of mixed race and multiracial children in Indiana, Iowa, South Dakota, and Mississippi has increased around 70 percent, while North Carolina's has more than doubled, and Georgia's has grown by more than 80 percent.[29]

_____

_____

_____

_____

_____

_____

Week 33 A budget bill was passed in Texas that requires public institutions that house centers for "alternative sexualities" to provide equal funding for new centers that focus on "traditional values." During the debate of this bill, lawmakers made jokes about gay, lesbian, homosexual, bisexual, pansexual, transsexual, transgender, gender questioning, and gender identity issues and community members.[30]

_____

_____

_____

_____

_____

_____

_____

Week 34 A transwoman's tenure was denied and she was terminated from her faculty position even though she had an overwhelming amount of support from her students and colleagues. Regardless of her outstanding scholarship and teaching record, the Dean and Vice President of Academic Affairs didn't reverse their decision.[31]

_____

_____

_____

_____

_____

_____

_____

_____

Week 35 After learning that the Obama administration used legendary Apache leader Geronimo to name the secret raid that lead to the killing of Osama bin Laden, Winona Ladue, Native American activist and writer, responded with the following statement: "The reality is that the military is full of native nomenclature... You've got Black Hawk helicopters, Apache Longbow helicopters, you've got Tomahawk missiles. The term used when you leave a military base in a foreign country is 'off the reservation into Indian Country.' So what is that messaging that's being passed on? Basically, it is the continuation of the wars against indigenous people." [32]

Week 36 People in a same-gender relationship can be considered "without blanket judgment" for ordination after a majority of the Presbyterian Church's 173 presbyteries ratified a constitutional amendment. [33]

_____

_____

_____

_____

_____

_____

_____

_____

_____

_____

Week 37 David Stocker and Kathy Witterick of Toronto, Canada, have decided to keep the sexual identity of their baby a secret. Only seven people know the identity of their four-month-old infant, Storm. Storm's two older brothers, Jazz and Kio, are allowed to wear pink and dress as girls.[34]

_____

_____

_____

_____

_____

_____

_____

_____

Week 38 *The Mikado,* an original yellow face opera, was produced in Austin, Texas, in June 2011 without a historical explanation of the racial implications of the original production.[35]

_____

_____

_____

_____

_____

_____

_____

_____

_____

_____

A self-identified obese student requests that her classrooms accommodate her size with moveable chairs and tables as a sitting option for everyone. She is not willing to have these accommodations through Disability Services. She doesn't want to be labeled as disabled and doesn't want to be singled out or segregated to a lone table with moveable chairs in the back of the room.

_____

_____

_____

_____

_____

_____

_____

A US Airways pilot called the police when a black passenger didn't immediately pull up his sagging pants as instructed upon boarding the flight. The 20-year-old passenger, Deshon Marman, who was returning from his best friend's funeral to attend classes at the University of New Mexico, pulled up his pants upon reaching his assigned seat. When confronted by the pilot and police, he stated that he was like everyone else on the plane. The pilot said, "No, you are not." Marman was arrested, handcuffed, and jailed. Prosecutors ended up not pressing charges, but US Airways stands by its pilot's behavior.[36]

_____

_____

_____

_____

_____

_____

Week 41 Fifteen-year-old Anthony Stewart of Syracuse, NY, was convicted of a felony and will serve 2-6 years in juvenile detention after being found guilty of first-degree robbery and beating a 73-year-old man. Stewart had a BB gun and took $.07 from the man after knocking him into a snow bank.[37]

_____

_____

_____

_____

_____

_____

_____

_____

Week 42 Thirty Bangladeshi factory workers were killed in a preventable factory fire at the sweatshop where they made sportswear that is sold at Abercrombie, Gap, and JCPenney.[38]

_____

_____

_____

_____

_____

_____

_____

_____

_____

_____

Week 43 Without physical evidence, Troy Davis was found guilty of murdering a police officer in Savannah, Georgia, in 1989 and was executed in 2011.[39]

_____

_____

_____

_____

_____

_____

_____

_____

_____

_____

Week 44 The University of California, Berkeley voted 19-0 against an Affirmative Action bake sale hosted by the Young Republicans, stating, "the use of discrimination whether it is in satire or in seriousness by any student group isn't acceptable." [40]

_____

_____

_____

_____

_____

_____

_____

_____

_____

Week 45 The first "Slut Walk" was organized in January 2011 to end Slut Shaming after a representative of the Toronto Police department stated, "Women should avoid dressing like sluts in order not to be victimized."[41]

_____

_____

_____

_____

_____

_____

_____

_____

_____

_____

Week 46 In Bangor, Maine, there is a race that gives the winner his wife's weight in beer. To win, you have to pick up your wife and run with her. In addition to beer, the winner also gets six times her weight in cash. [42]

_____

_____

_____

_____

_____

_____

_____

_____

_____

_____

Week 47 An average of 700 Native American children are removed from homes each year and placed into foster care in South Dakota. These children make up only 15 percent of the children in the state but over half of those in foster care. State records show that nearly 90 percent of these children are placed in non-native homes or group care systems.[43]

_____

_____

_____

_____

_____

_____

_____

_____

Week 48 Although hate crimes are often underreported, between 2009 and 2010 those hate crimes that were reported in Phoenix rose by 40 percent. Of the 135 reported, 50 were classified as race-related, 37 involved sexual orientation, 27 were over ethnicity, 19 involved religion, and two involved hate crimes based on disability.[44]

Week 49 *Forbes* editors received an unexpected amount of reaction to an article called, "If I Was a Poor Black Kid," that offers free educational tools and focuses on training in technical areas of interest.[45]

_____

_____

_____

_____

_____

_____

_____

_____

_____

_____

Week 50 "I'm not a bad person," states Jamie Hein of Cincinnati after being accused of discrimination by an African American girl because she has a 1931 sign from Alabama posted at her swimming pool. The sign reads, "Public Swimming Pool, White Only." [46]

_____

_____

_____

_____

_____

_____

_____

_____

_____

Week 51 A white graduate student from Rutgers University's English Department's course, "Post-Bellum/Pre-Harlem," sends an email invitation for a whites-only screening of Walt Disney's 1946 film, *Song of the South*.[47]

_____

_____

_____

_____

_____

_____

_____

_____

_____

_____

Week 52 While running for President, former Senator Rick Santorum (R-PA) said to Republicans in Iowa that his administration would not offer welfare at all. He added, "I don't want to make black people's lives better by giving them other people's money. I want to give them the opportunity to go out and earn their money and provide for themselves and their families." [48]

Next week... You have had a year's worth of practice! Congratulations. Continue your own self-reflection. Encourage others to do similar work. This is the only way to work through the inherited privilege of our dominant identities. Look forward to future editions of *Notice Notes!*

_____

_____

_____

_____

_____

_____

_____

_____

_____

_____

_____

_____

_____

_____

_____

_____

_____

_____

Notice something? Feel free to email Jess at Jess@iamsocialjustice.com with your own noticings for possible inclusion in future editions of *Notice Notes*. Submission does not guarantee inclusion and entries may be edited by author.

Endnotes

[1] The concept of Noticing pulls from trainings and readings using terms like Tracking and Panning. The source of these training and readings cite their work as adapted from materials developed by Elsie Y. Cross Associates, Inc. 1994 Delyte Frost, et al., and the Social Justice Leadership Institute's Core Curriculum (www.sjti.org).

[2] http://www.utsandiego.com/news/2010/feb/26/noose-protest-ucsd/, February 26, 2010

Here is the link to the "apology" from the student responsible for leaving a noose in the library: http://www.newuniversity .org/2010/03/opinion/opinioneater/apology-from-ucsd-student-about-the-noose/, March 1, 2010

Here is also a link for an agreement signed by UCSD and the Black Student Union: http://www.ucsdnews.ucsd.edu/ newsrel/general/03-04agreement.asp, March 4, 2012

[3] http://www.theaggie.org/2010/02/26/letter-lgbtrc-vandal ized/, February 26, 2010

[4] http://www.gay.pinknews.co.uk/2010/03/11/australia-is-first-to-recognise-non-specified-gender/, March 11, 2010

[5] http://www.racebending.com/v3/press/racebending-face book-group-taken-down/, March 15, 2010

For more information visit http://www.racebending.com/ v3/about/

[6] http://www.postandcourier.com/article/20100311/PC1602/303119909, March 11, 2010

Here is a link to the Supreme Court's ultimate decision: http://www.pennlive.com/midstate/index.ssf/2011/03/westboro_baptist_church_vs_mar.html, March 3, 2010

[7] http://www.sfgate.com/education/article/UC-regents-sorry-for-acts-of-hate-on-campuses-3269495.php, March 25, 2010

[8] http://thegrio.com/2010/04/16/obama-extends-health-care-rights-to-gay-partners/, April 16, 2010

[9] http://www.chicoer.com/news/ci_14912583, April 19, 2010

[10] http://www.nytimes.com/2010/04/24/us/politics/24immig.html?_r=0, April 24, 2010

[11] http://www.presstelegram.com/news/ci_14948962, April 23, 2010

[12] http://www.foxnews.com/politics/2010/04/30/arizona-legislature-passes-banning-ethnic-studies-programs/, April 30, 2010

[13] http://www.huffingtonpost.com/2010/04/30/arizona-ethnic-studies-cl_n_558731.html, April 30, 2010

[14] http://www.weac.org/news_and_publications/10-05-06/Governor_Doyle_signs_race-based_school_mascot_logo_bill_into_law.aspx, May 6, 2010

[15] http://www.statesman.com/news/news/local/ut-system-regents-vote-to-rename-simkins-hall/nRwKc/, July 15, 2010

[16] http://www.genderacrossborders.com/2010/05/11/american-apparel-american-able-girl-next-door/, May 11, 2010

[17] http://pediatrics.aappublications.org/content/125/5/1088.full, May 5, 2010

[18] http://www.azcentral.com/news/articles/2010/06/04/201 00604arizona-mural-sparks-racial-debate.html, June 4, 2010

For more information visit: http://wonkette.com/415809/arizona-school-demands-black-latino-students-faces-on-mural-be-changed-to-white, July 22, 2010

[19] http://electronicintifada.net/content/you-will-have-no-protection/8862, June 4, 2010

[20] http://www.huffingtonpost.com/2010/05/27/my-ex-wifes-wedding-dress_n_591621.html#s94001&title=Dog_Toy_, May 27, 2010

[21] http://www.theatlantic.com/magazine/archive/2010/07/rent-a-white-guy/308119/, June 8, 2010

For more information visit: http://www.npr.org/templates/story/story.php?storyId=128011084, June 22, 2010

[22] http://www.insidehighered.com/news/2010/06/28/supreme, June 28, 2010

[23] This posted to a listserv in July of 2010; as of 2/3/2013 it doesn't exist anymore — but I thought it was still interesting. Here is the original link: http://www1.csbsju.edu/mens center/default.htm; I conducted a search of the university's website but found nothing.

24 http://www.cnn.com/2010/US/05/19/doll.study.reactions/index.html, May 19, 2010

25 http://www.nytimes.com/2010/12/02/sports/golf/02lpga.html, December 1, 2010

   For original story visit: http://www.myfoxtampabay.com/story/18022745/transgender-golfer-sues-lpga-in-bid-to-join-tour, October 13, 2010

26 http://www.miamistudent.net/opinion/indian-party-elevates-racial-tension-1.1777613#.UQ7n-GeS-So, November 15, 2010

27 http://www.mnn.com/food/healthy-eating/blogs/in-denver-everyone-can-afford-to-eat-organic, February 28, 2011

28 http://www.npr.org/templates/story/story.php?storyId=134623120, March 17, 2011

   A 2011 study shows that white students receive significantly more scholarships and grants: http://colorlines.com/archives/2011/09/study_shows_that_white_students_are_more_likely_to_get_scholarship_money.html, September 12, 2011

29 http://www.nytimes.com/2011/03/20/us/20race.html?_r=1&partner=rss&emc=rss, March 20, 2011

   For the direct link to the Census Bureau visit: http://www.census.gov/#

30 http://www.insidehighered.com/news/2011/04/25/texas_house_votes_to_require_colleges_with_sexuality_centers_to_promote_traditional_values_too, April 25, 2011

[31] http://chronicle.com/blognetwork/tenuredradical/2011/04/from-bathrooms-to-board-rooms-is-being/, April 24, 2011

[32] http://www.democracynow.org/2011/5/6/native_american_activist_winona_laduke_on, April 6, 2011

[33] http://library.constantcontact.com/download/get/file/1102583984837-127/presbytery_news.pdf, May 10, 2011

[34] http://www2.ljworld.com/weblogs/at-random/2011/may/26/baby-storm-is-gender-freedom-abuse-or-bl/, May 26, 2011

[35] http://newredindian.wordpress.com/2011/06/15/austins-no-place-for-yellow-face/, June 15, 2011

[36] http://act.colorofchange.org/sign/usairways, June 18, 2011

[37] http://www.cbsnews.com/8301-504083_162-20099378-504083.html, August 30, 2011

[38] http://www.change.org/petitions/jc-penney-dont-break-your-promise-to-families-of-workers-who-died-making-your-clothes?utm_source=action_alert&utm_medium=email&alert_id=rQanerDeCt_xjTTgTayFj, October 2011

[39] https://secure2.convio.net/ip/site/Advocacy?page=UserActionInactive&id=227, September 21, 2011

For more information, visit: http://www.amnestyusa.org/our-work/cases/usa-troy-davis

[40] http://www.npr.org/blogs/thetwo-way/2011/09/26/140809070/gop-students-race-based-bake-sale-sparks-controversy-at-berkeley, September 26, 2011

[41] http://www.slutwalktoronto.com/, July 24, 2011

A picture is on facebook of a similar walk in NYC showing a white woman in a bikini top holding a sign with the "N" word on display: https://www.facebook.com/photo.php?fbid=236901013025305&set=a.236900106358729.54390.100001162236286&type=1&theater, October 4, 2011

This sign is referencing a John Lennon song. For a fabulous critique of the Slut Walk through a white privilege lens visit: http://www.peopleofcolororganize.com/activism/slutwalk-whiteness-privilege-sex-trafficking-women-color/ (As of 7/22/2013, this site is under maintenance.)

[42] http://beerstreetjournal.com/carry-your-wife-win-her-weight-in-beer/, October 9, 2011

[43] http://www.npr.org/2011/10/25/141662357/incentives-and-cultural-bias-fuel-foster-system, October 25, 2011

[44] http://www.azcentral.com/community/phoenix/articles/2011/11/16/20111116phoenix-racial-hate-crimes-surge.html, November 16, 2011

[45] http://www.forbes.com/sites/quickerbettertech/2011/12/12/if-i-was-a-poor-black-kid/, December 12, 2011

One of many responses: http://www.balloon-juice.com/2011/12/13/if-i-were-a-poor-black-kid/, December 13, 2011

Here are more that are posted on the Forbes site: http://www.forbes.com/sites/kashmirhill/2011/12/14/trolling-the-internet-with-if-i-were-a-poor-black-kid/, December 14, 2011

http://www.theatlantic.com/national/archive/2011/12/a-muscular-empathy/249984/, December 2011

http://www.dominionofnewyork.com/2011/12/13/if-i-were-the-middle-class-white-guy-gene-marks/#.Tuj7B7Ik67v, December 13, 2011

http://www.good.is/post/an-ode-to-a-poor-black-kid-i-never-knew-how-forbes-gets-it-wrong/, December 13, 2011

[46] http://abcnews.go.com/blogs/headlines/2011/12/exclusive-white-only-pool-sign-owner-explains/, December 15, 2011

[47] http://www.dailymail.co.uk/news/article-2075387/Rutgers-University-outrage-email-whites-movie-screening.html#ixzz1gp3P8aCu, December 17, 2011

[48] http://www.rawstory.com/rs/2012/01/02/santorum-tells-iowans-i-dont-want-to-make-black-peoples-lives-better/, January 2, 2012

From the moment you meet Jessica, you know you're in for something that will challenge your mind, inspire your conscience, and invigorate you to pursue change in your community. Nominated three times by *Campus Activities Magazine* for Best Diversity Artist and referred to as the "Margaret Cho" of diversity trainers, Jessica's programs are direct, customized, and highly interactive. Her workshops, seminars, and keynotes don't just leave participants energized, but also inspired and motivated to follow through with action to create change. Jessica uses her take on life to lead participants through a safe, but confrontational, process of examination, self-reflection, and open dialog that is as challenging as it is rewarding.

Remember, you are your best learning and teaching tool. Keep your best tools sharp. Always use the best tools. Trust the process. Listen to yourself. Listen to others. Breathe. Grow.

Getting There!

In addition to joining Jess's monthly conference call, **Go There!**, why not host your own?

The idea started as a campus-based conversation and moved to a free national conference call to discuss current events. Now you can use the **Getting There! Facilitation Guide** to keep the sharing going. Your campus can host a Go There! and you can invite your folks to be on Jess's calls — it is a win-win for all!

For information about the next Go There! conference call — check out Jess's newsletter, Another Isolated Incident, for the upcoming dial-in information.

www.jessicapettitt.com/gothere

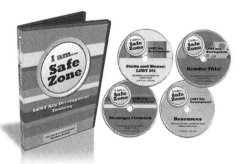

Now that you have conversation practice it is time for application: **I am... Safe Zone: LGBT Ally Development Training DVDs + Resource Disc** ties together different systems of oppression and views them through the lens of sex, and sexual and gender identity. Watch three interactive workshops, use the included facilitator guides to write or update your own Safe Zone curriculum, or use this material to renew and jumpstart your Ally Development program(s) to be more inclusive of other subordinated identities. Also, check out the website for upcoming drive-in live trainings or host your own!

www.iamsafezone.com

Jess's one stop shop for social justice, diversity, LGBT, and Trans-inclusion resources, trainings, keynotes, and resources primarily targeted to colleges and universities. Download publications, assessment tools, and articles; watch videos; and/or book Jess to speak and facilitate tough conversations in your organization.

www.iamsocialjustice.com

Want to keep Jess in your pocket? Download this **free iPhone or Android-based app** and connect to Jess's website, blog, facebook, calendar, and random thoughts. You can also leave comments and post pictures of her in action!

www.jessicapettitt.com/buy

anotherisolatedincident

Another Isolated Incident is a **monthly newsletter** of resources, reflections on current events, Go There! call-in information, and a link to Jess's calendar. Short, sweet, and to the point, we all need to take a minute to realize that of the many isolated incidents — many are just repetitive patterns covering systems of oppression that we need to dismantle. Together — we can do anything — but we can't do everything.

www.jessicapettitt.com/newsletter

not so isolated... not so random...

I am... Jessica Pettitt

I am... Social Justice

my experience of social justice work

Not so isolated… not so random… is a bi-weekly (or so) glimpse into Jess's world, experiences, thoughts, feelings, and observations. One reader describes the **blog** by stating, "Jess shows just enough skin to keep me motivated to do the hard work without seeing my results. We are in this together."

www.jessicapettitt.com/blog

The lighter side of inclusion work is about having fun! **Jess can emcee your next meeting or event** and take the pressure off of the planning committee. You have done the planning — now enjoy what you have created and let your emcee introduce, connect, transition, keep time, and help participants love the event. Anyone can host an event — but only a few go the extra mile and provide the **Shebango!** that people talk about. This word of mouth ties directly to membership recruitment, retention, and return on investment of participants.

www.shebango.com

**To order additional copies of this book,
Notice Notes, or Notice Notes III**

visit Amazon.com or

www.jessicapettitt.com/notice-notes

Also available:

**Notice Notes: A <Huge>
Facilitation Guide to Stir Up
Conversations**

This valuable resource includes
syllabi, teacher's guides, and
programming plans so that you
can choose how to use these tools.

Ten percent of all proceeds from the sales of Notice Notes will
be given to the Social Justice Training Institute, Inc., a 501(c)(3)
organization, to continue and support the work done in the
professional institutes, student experiences, drive-in trainings,
and other community initiatives.

Made in the USA
San Bernardino, CA
10 November 2015